NOW YOU CAN READ....
Three Little Pigs

STORY ADAPTED BY LUCY KINCAID

ILLUSTRATED BY ERIC ROWE

BRIMAX BOOKS • CAMBRIDGE • ENGLAND

Once upon a time there were three little pigs. One day, their mother said, "You are old enough to look after yourselves now. It is time for you to go out into the world and build homes of your own."

The three little pigs were very excited. They walked together as far as the crossroads and there they parted.

"Goodbye!" they called to one another as they set off in different directions.

The first little pig always did
things in a hurry. He built himself
a house of straw in the first sunny
field he came to. It was light
and airy and smelt of harvest time
and it swayed gently whenever the

wind blew.
One day he saw a
wicked old wolf
walking across the
field.

"OOOH!" cried the
first little pig
and ran inside his
house of straw.
The wolf knocked
at the door and
called, "Open the
door little pig
and let me in."
He wanted the
little pig for
his dinner.

The first little pig shivered and shook. "By the hair on my chinny chin chin, I will NOT open the door and let you come in."
"Then I will HUFF and I will PUFF and I will blow your house down," growled the wolf.

And he HUFFED and he PUFFED until the house of straw blew away. And THAT was the end of the first little pig.

The second little pig never quite finished anything he started. He built himself a house of sticks in a shady wood. It was full of gaps and creaked whenever the wind blew.

One day he saw a wicked old wolf walking along the woodland path. "OOOH!" cried the second little pig and ran inside his house of sticks. The wolf knocked at the door and called, "Open the door little pig and let me in." He wanted the little pig for his dinner.

The second little pig shivered and shook. "By the hair on my chinny chin chin, I will NOT open the door and let you come in."

"Then I will HUFF and I will PUFF and I will blow your house down," growled the wolf.
And he HUFFED and he PUFFED until the house of sticks tumbled down. And THAT was the end of the second little pig.

The third little
pig always did
everything properly,
even if it took
him a long time.
He built a house
of bricks at the
bottom of a steep
hill. It was snug
and warm and stood
firm and strong.

One day he saw a wicked old wolf walking down the hill.

"OOOH!" cried the third little pig and ran inside his house of bricks. The wolf knocked at the door and called, "Open the door little pig and let me in." He wanted the little pig for his dinner.

The third little pig shivered and shook. "By the hair on my chinny chin chin, I will NOT open the door and let you come in."
"Then I will HUFF and I will PUFF and I will blow your house down," growled the wolf.

And he HUFFED and he PUFFED and then he HUFFED and PUFFED again.

The wicked old wolf HUFFED and he PUFFED until he was quite out of breath but the house of bricks stood as firm and as strong as a mountain. He could NOT blow it down. If he wanted to catch the little pig he would have to entice him out of the house.

"Little pig," he called. "Meet me in the orchard at ten o'clock tomorrow morning and I will show you where the best apples are."

The third little pig knew how crafty and full of tricks the old wolf was so the next morning he got up very early. He went to the orchard and picked all the best apples and was safely home again by ten o'clock.

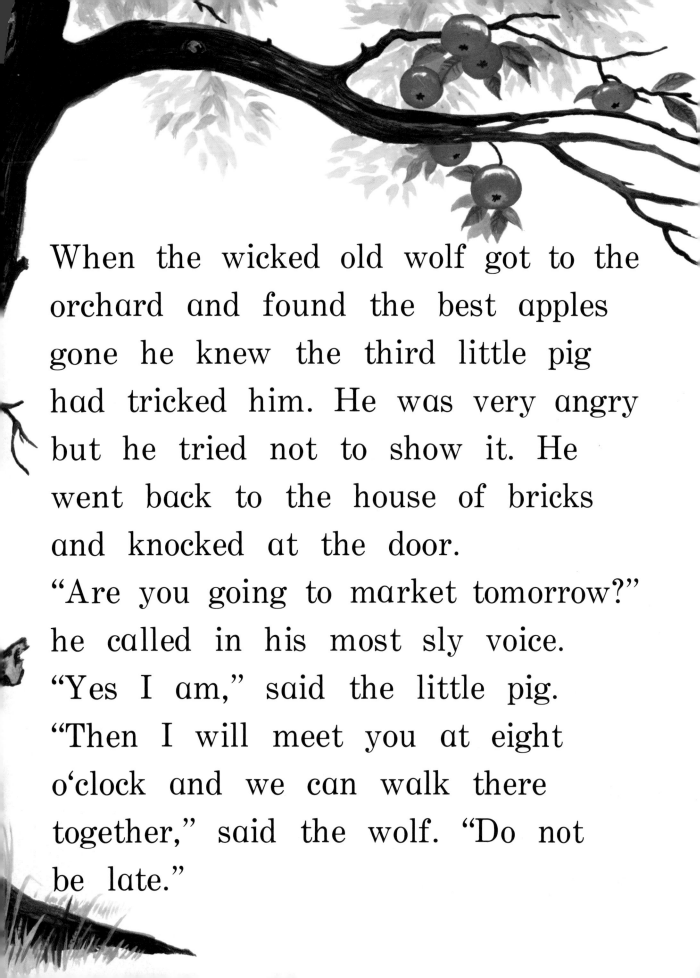

When the wicked old wolf got to the orchard and found the best apples gone he knew the third little pig had tricked him. He was very angry but he tried not to show it. He went back to the house of bricks and knocked at the door.

"Are you going to market tomorrow?" he called in his most sly voice.

"Yes I am," said the little pig.

"Then I will meet you at eight o'clock and we can walk there together," said the wolf. "Do not be late."

The third little pig got up very early indeed the next morning. "I will be home from market before the old wolf is even awake," he said. But he was wrong because the wolf got up early too.

The little pig was very frightened when he saw the wolf coming up the hill and he hid inside an empty milk churn which was standing beside the road.

The milk churn began to roll. It rolled down the hill. Faster and faster and faster. It bumped right into the old wolf and sent him sprawling.

"OOOH!" cried the wolf. He could not believe his eyes when he saw the little pig hop from the milk churn and run into the house of bricks and slam the door.

He was very angry indeed. If he could not catch the little pig outside the house then he would have to get into the house. If the little pig would not let him in through the door then he would go down the chimney.

The third little pig heard the wolf scrambling about on the roof.

"That wicked wolf will NEVER catch me," he cried. He put a pot full of water on the fire and waited. The rumbling and grumbling in the chimney got louder and then suddenly there was a great BIG SPLASH! The wicked old wolf had fallen straight into the pot. And THAT was the end of HIM.

And the third little pig lived happily ever after.

All these appear in the pages
of the story. Can you find them?

three little pigs

wolf

house of straw

house of sticks